SUPER COOL
CONSTRUCTION
ACTIVITIES
WITH Max Axiom

by Tammy Enz

Consultant:
Morgan Hynes, Ph.D.
Assistant Professor, Engineering Education

D1078809

Raintree is an imprint of Capstone Global Library Limited, a company incorporated in England and Wales having its registered office at 7 Pilgrim Street, London, EC4V 6LB – Registered company number: 6695582

www.raintree.co.uk
myorders@raintree.co.uk

Editorial Credits
Christopher L. Harbo, editor; Nathan Gassman, art director; Tracy McCabe, designer; Katy Lavigne, production specialist; Sarah Schuette and Marcy Morin, project creation

Cover Illustration
Marcelo Baez

Photo Credits
Photographs by Capstone Studio: Karon Dubke

ISBN 978 1 4062 9323 4 (hardback)
18 17 16 15 14
10 9 8 7 6 5 4 3 2 1

ISBN 978 1 4062 9328 9 (paperback)
19 18 17 16
10 9 8 7 6 5 4 3 2 1

British Library Cataloguing in Publication Data
A full catalogue record for this book is available from the British Library.

Printed in China

Contents

Ah-ha! It looks like clay is the clear winner. The soil is quickly crumbling and the water is pouring through the rock...

...as my action figure just found out.

But that's OK. Building small-scale construction projects allows us to test what works and what doesn't work before building the real thing.

Get ready to exercise your engineering skills. A host of construction projects await!

LEVEE

It's your turn to build a levee. These large structures are built on a river's **flood plain** to protect homes and cities. Engineers often combine different materials to improve a levee's strength. Construct your own levee design with a few simple supplies.

YOU'LL NEED

egg box

scissors

large container with a smooth bottom

gravel

sand

water

modelling clay

rolling pin

PLAN OF ACTION

1. Using the scissors, cut off four or five egg cups from the egg box. Place these upside down on one side of the large container. They represent buildings on a flood plain.

2. Create a wall of gravel 5 to 7 centimetres high along the middle of the container.

3. Mix a small amount of water with the sand to make it damp. Pack sand around the gravel wall.

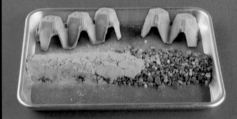

4. Roll and pat the clay into a flat sheet long enough and wide enough to cover the wall. Place the sheet over the wall. Smooth it and press its edges to the sides and bottom of the container to form a tight seal. This is your levee.

5. Slowly fill the side of the container opposite the egg cups with water to represent rising floodwaters.

6. Note areas where the levee is weak or leaky. Apply more gravel to make parts of the levee stronger. Add clay to fill in leaks.

AXIOM ALTERNATIVE

Engineers use fabrics called geotextiles to prevent soil from washing away during floods. Try wrapping your levee with pieces from a mesh fruit bag to act like a geotextile. Does the fruit bag strengthen the levee?

flood plain area of low land near a stream or river that becomes flooded during periods of heavy rain

 ARCH

In ancient times, builders often built stone arches without using cement. How did they do this? The secret is the keystone at the very top of an arch. This wedge-shaped stone holds all the pieces together. Test out the keystone concept with a simple foam arch.

YOU'LL NEED

46-cm square of 5-cm-thick foam

electric foam cutter

ruler

pencil

SAFETY FIRST

Ask an adult for permission to use an electric foam cutter before starting this project.

PLAN OF ACTION

1. Cut a 13-cm square from the foam.

2. Measure and mark a spot 4 cm in from one corner of the square. Draw a line from this mark to the opposite corner of the square. Cut along the line to make a truncated triangle.

3. Repeat steps 1 and 2 to make a second identical shape.

4. Draw a trapezium on the remaining foam. Make it 5 cm along the base, 4 cm along its top, and 2.5 cm high. Cut out this shape.

5. Repeat step 4 four more times to make additional trapeziums with the same dimensions.

6. Set the truncated triangles upright so they sit about 11 cm apart. These triangles will be the supports for the arch.

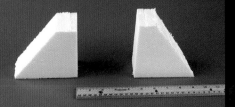

7. Begin stacking the slanted edges of the trapeziums onto the supports to begin forming an arch shape. Stack two on each support, holding them in place as you stack.

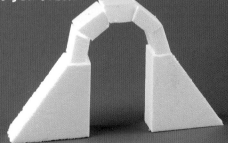

8. Ask a friend to place the final trapezium, the "keystone", between the stacks to finish the arch and lock the blocks into place.

AXIOM ALTERNATIVE

Make additional foam blocks and build a bridge or a span of connected arches. Try doubling or tripling the dimensions of your foam blocks to make larger arches and structures. How tall can you make your arch?

truncate shorten by cutting off the top of an object

trapezium shape with four sides, only two of which are parallel

MOTORWAY RAMP

Many busy cities around the world have a network of roads and ramps twisting and weaving around and through each other. Transportation engineers design circular ramps so drivers can safely enter and exit busy roads and motorways. These ramps must allow cars to make tight turns without crashing or spinning off the road. Test out your engineering skills by building a motorway ramp to keep a marble on a safe course.

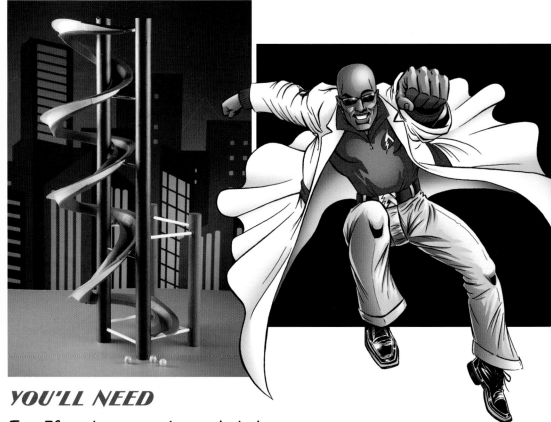

YOU'LL NEED

Two 76-cm-long wrapping paper tubes

ruler

sharpened pencil

11 unsharpened pencils

Two 30-cm-long kitchen roll tubes

hot glue gun

12 sturdy paper plates

scissors

packing tape

marble

SAFETY FIRST

Ask an adult for permission to use a hot glue gun before starting this project.

PLAN OF ACTION

1. Measure and mark 2.5 cm, 23 cm, 43 cm, 58 cm and 73 cm from one end of a wrapping paper tube. Use a sharpened pencil to poke a hole at each of these marks. Repeat this step with the other wrapping paper tube.

2. Insert unsharpened pencils into the holes made in step 1 to connect the tubes.

3. Mark 2.5 cm from each end of both kitchen roll tubes. Connect them as in step 2.

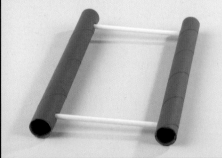

4. Lay the smaller rectangle flat on the floor. Poke holes on the top faces of the tubes, 90 degrees from the first holes. These holes will be perpendicular to the pencils holding the rectangle together. Insert an unsharpened pencil into each of these holes.

5. Stand the small and large rectangles next to each other. Mark spots where the pencils in the small rectangle touch the large rectangle. Punch holes at these locations on the large rectangle and insert the unsharpened pencil ends to make a tower.

perpendicular describes two lines that intersect at a 90-degree angle; two lines that form the letter T are perpendicular to each other

6. Adjust the pencils and tubes to make the tower square. Use hot glue to secure the pencils in place.

7. Cut the outside rims from the paper plates. Leave only 1 cm of the flat centre of the plate. Cut away the rest of the plate and discard.

8. Turn one rim upside down and lay it on top of another rim to form a trough. Tape the rims to each other on their undersides. Continue taping rims together to form a long trough coil. This is your ramp.

9. Tape one end of the coil to the highest pencil on the tower. Begin winding it around one of the wrapping paper tubes. Test each curve by rolling a marble on it to make sure the marble can travel along the curve without flying off. Tape the coil to the tube as you move your way down the structure, constantly testing your ramp.

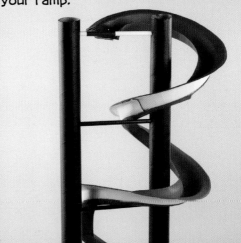

10. When the ramp reaches the ground, test the entire structure by rolling a marble from top to bottom. Adjust the ramp as needed so that the marble rolls all the way down.

⚡ **AXIOM ALTERNATIVE**

Construct another spiralling ramp. Attach it to the other wrapping paper tube and connect the ramps. Then race marbles on each of the ramps, trying not to crash them.

trough long, narrow channel

SUSPENSION BRIDGE

Suspension bridges use anchored cables to carry the weight of their bridge decks. They are famous for spanning larger gaps than other types of bridge. They easily span distances from 600 to 2,100 metres. Prepare to experience the awesome engineering behind the suspension bridge.

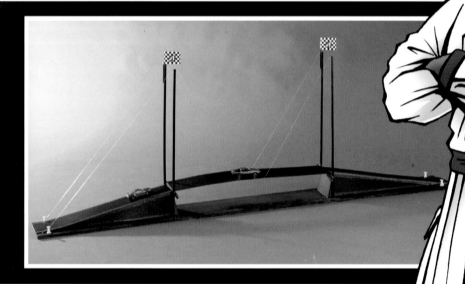

YOU'LL NEED

86-cm x 11-cm piece of plywood

ruler

pencil

drill

5-mm drill bit

4 wooden skewers

utility knife

hot glue gun

2 wooden craft sticks

tape

32-cm x 8-cm piece of paper

4 drawing pins

Two 1.5 metre-long pieces of fishing line

empty cardboard cereal box

scissors

toy car

an adult to help you!

PLAN OF ACTION

1. Measure and draw lines 1 cm in from each of the plywood's long edges. Measuring from a short edge of the plywood, make marks at 2.5 cm, 28 cm, 58 cm and 84 cm on both lines. Ask an adult to drill holes at each of these marks.

2. With an adult's help, use the utility knife to slice a 1-cm slit into the blunt ends of each of the skewers.

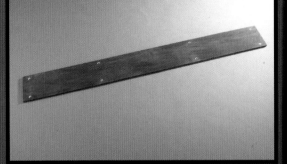

3. Insert the pointed end of each skewer into each of the four centre-most holes in the plywood. Rotate the skewers so the slits are parallel to the long sides of the plywood. Secure the skewers in place with hot glue.

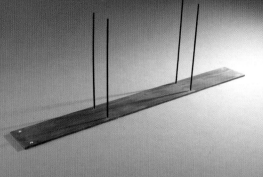

4. Measure and mark 5 cm up from the bottom of each upright skewer. Place the top edge of a craft stick across each set of skewers at this mark. Glue the craft sticks in place to make two H shapes.

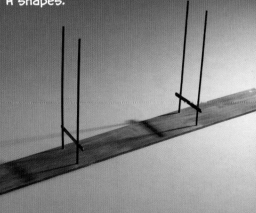

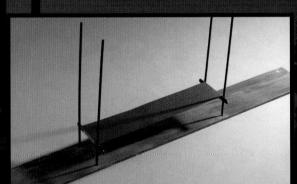

5. Measure and mark a line 5 mm from each short end of the paper strip. Fold the paper at these marks and unfold halfway. Hang the folded edges over the craft sticks. Tape the edges to the craft sticks to make the bridge deck.

6. Firmly push a pin into each of the remaining holes on the piece of plywood.

7. Wrap and tie one end of a piece of fishing line around one of the drawing pins. Thread it up through the slit on the nearest upright and under the centre of the paper deck.

8. Tape the fishing line to the underside of the paper and then continue threading it through the slit in the adjoining upright. Wrap and tie the end of the line around the adjacent drawing pin. Make sure the fishing line is pulled taut, but the deck remains flat.

9. Repeat steps 7 and 8 at the opposite end of the bridge.

10. Lay the cereal box flat. Measure and mark 5 cm from one corner along the bottom of the box. Measure and mark 25.5 cm from this corner along the side of the box. Draw a straight line between these points. Flip the box and repeat. Cut along these lines to form a wedge.

11. Repeat step 10 with the other bottom corner of the box. Place the wedges at either end of the bridge to form ramped abutments.

12. Place a toy car on the bridge to see the suspension cables tighten to hold its weight.

⚡ AXIOM ALTERNATIVE

Experiment with different bridge deck materials. Can you get a cellophane bridge deck to work? Does a cardboard deck make a stronger bridge?

parallel side by side at an equal distance between all points

abutment part of a structure that directly receives thrust or pressure

WASTE WATER TREATMENT PLANT

Have you ever wondered what happens to waste water when you flush the toilet or drain a sink? Construct a simple two-tank **septic system** to separate solids and to clean liquids before returning water to the environment.

YOU'LL NEED

2-litre drinks bottle

ruler

marker

utility knife

4-pint plastic milk carton

36-cm x 20-cm piece of plywood

2 drinking straws

hot glue gun

25-cm-long
2 x 4 board

2 cotton balls

clean sand

clean gravel

small dish

muddy water

SAFETY FIRST

Ask an adult to help you with the utility knife and hot glue gun before starting this project.

septic system drainage system with a tank used to treat waste water

PLAN OF ACTION

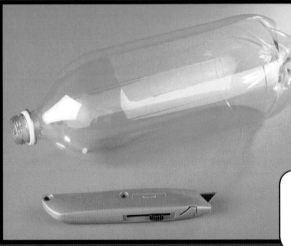

1. Draw an oval that is about 5 cm wide by 13 cm long on the 2-litre bottle. The oval should start at the bottom of one of the bottle's feet. Ask an adult to cut the oval out with the utility knife.

2. Lay the milk carton on its side. Ask an adult to cut out a large square from its top side using the utility knife.

3. Lay the two straws 5 cm apart on the plywood. One end of each straw should be even with one of the plywood's short sides. Secure the straws in place with hot glue.

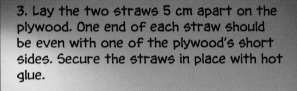

4. Lay the 2-litre bottle between the two straws with the oval hole on top. Make its bottom even with the straw ends.

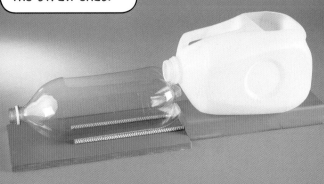

5. Place one end of the 2 x 4 board behind the bottom of the 2-litre bottle. Lay the milk carton on the board with its hole facing up. Allow the carton's spout to overlap the 2-litre bottle's oval hole.

continued

6. Stuff the cotton balls tightly into the neck of the 2-litre bottle.

7. Pack sand into the front end of the bottle, nearest the cotton balls.

8. Fill the rest of the bottle with gravel.

9. Place the dish under the neck of the bottle.

10. Slowly pour muddy water into the hole of the milk carton.

11. Watch as the solids in the water sink to the bottom of the carton. The rest of the water will begin flowing into the drinks bottle to be cleaned by the gravel and sand. It will exit the system as clean water. Continue pouring in muddy water.

Each time the water level reaches the level of the spout, it will trickle into the gravel. (Although the exiting water looks clean, do not drink it because the system will not remove all the bacteria and chemicals.)

12. Rinse out the solids in the first tank (milk carton) as it begins to fill up.

AXIOM ALTERNATIVE

In a real-life septic system, solids are pumped out as the tank fills up. Design a system to pump out the solids as they collect in the first tank. A hose with a large syringe for a pump might do the job.

HYDRAULIC DRAWBRIDGE

A traffic bridge crossing a shipping channel can pose big problems for ships that are too large to pass under it. Engineers have designed the perfect solution – the drawbridge. A drawbridge lifts and lowers to allow ships to pass under it. See how it works with this hydraulic-powered drawbridge.

YOU'LL NEED

3 wooden skewers

ruler

pencil

scissors

4 cardboard toilet roll tubes

sharp nail

8 large wooden craft sticks

hot glue gun

2 small curtain wire eyelet screws

27-cm x 14-cm piece of cardboard

2 syringes

30-cm-long plastic hose with a 3-mm inside diameter

SAFETY FIRST

Ask an adult for permission to use a hot glue gun before starting this project.

PLAN OF ACTION

1. Measure and mark 11 cm from the blunt end of each of the skewers. Clip off this section with scissors and discard the rest of the skewer.

2. Measure and mark 1 cm from one end of two cardboard tubes. Poke holes through these marks with the sharp nail. Insert a skewer into the hole in one of the tubes. Stick the other end of the skewer into the hole in the other tube.

3. Measure and make two marks on each of the remaining tubes. Make them 1 cm from one of the ends and 1 cm apart. Punch poles at these marks and connect the tubes with two parallel skewers.

4. Trim one rounded end from six of the craft sticks with scissors.

5. Lay three sticks from step 4 side-by-side with their square ends even. Repeat with the three remaining sticks. Bring the square ends together.

6. Measure and cut 5-cm sections from the remaining sticks. Lay one 5-cm segment across the join between the sets of sticks. Glue in place. Lay the remaining 5-cm pieces about 2.5 cm from either end of the sticks. Glue in place to finish the bridge deck.

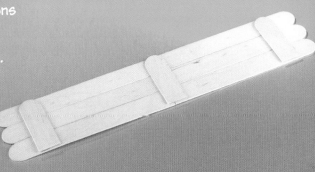

7. Screw the eyelet screws into the centre of one of the 5-cm end pieces on the bridge deck. Space the eyelets about 4 cm apart. Make sure the screws don't pierce the other side of the sticks.

8. Slide out one end of the skewer from the tubes connected in step 2. Thread the eyelets onto the skewer and replace the cardboard tube.

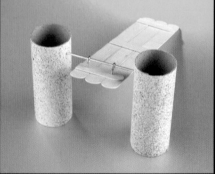

9. Place the whole bridge structure on top of the piece of cardboard. Align the tubes at each corner so that their edges are even with the sides of the cardboard. Glue in place.

10. Insert each of the syringe tips into either end of the hose. Remove one of the syringe's plungers. Close the plunger on the other syringe. With a friend's help, fill the empty syringe with water.

Then pull the other syringe's plunger to fill the hose and syringe with water. Place the plunger back into the empty syringe. Adjust the syringes so that as one opens, the other closes.

11. Insert the back end of one syringe between the skewers from step 3. Allow the syringe's flanges to rest on skewers along the centre of their span. Glue the flanges in place.

12. Push and pull the other plunger to raise and lower the bridge.

flange lip or edge that sticks out from something

NEWSPAPER PYRAMID

When the Egyptians built the pyramids, they chose a shape they thought would stand the test of time. But why have these structures lasted for thousands of years? As well as being built from stone, a pyramid's wide base and narrow peak is incredibly stable. Test the strength and stability of a pyramid with a structure made only from newspaper and tape.

YOU'LL NEED

newspaper (30 to 40 sheets)

packing tape

ruler

scissors

stapler

pencil

PLAN OF ACTION

1. Lay two sheets of newspaper side-by-side with their short sides touching. Tape the short sides together using long strips of packing tape.

3. Cut about 13 cm from each end of the tube. Wrap a piece of packing tape around each end to strengthen it.

4. Repeat steps 1 to 3 to make three more tubes. Make them the same length as the first tube.

2. Tightly roll the sheets diagonally into a tube. Tape the loose corner to keep the tube rolled.

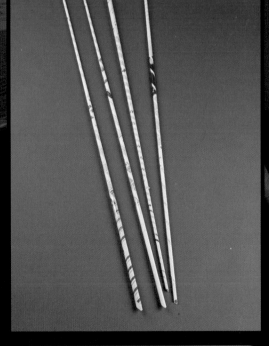

5. Lay three sheets of newspaper side-by-side with their short sides touching. Tape and roll them into a tube using the method outlined in steps 1 and 2. Then cut 13 cm off each end of the tube.

continued

6. Repeat step 5 to create three more tubes. Make each of these tubes the same length as the tube in that step.

7. Lay the short tubes in a square shape with their ends overlapping.

8. Staple the ends together to make the base of the pyramid.

10. Stand up the long tubes and staple their ends together over the centre of the square to form the framework of the pyramid.

9. Staple one end of each longer tube to one of the base's corners. Make sure the other end of each long tube angles diagonally inwards towards the centre of the square.

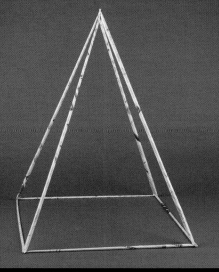

11. Lay several pieces of newspaper side-by-side to form a sheet large enough to cover one side of the pyramid. Tape the papers together.

13. Wrap the newspaper triangle around the tubes and tape it in place.

12. Lay one side of the pyramid on the top of the newspaper sheets. Trace the outline of the triangle about 2.5 cm larger than the triangle on each side. Cut along these lines.

14. Repeat steps 10 to 12 to cover two additional sides of the pyramid.

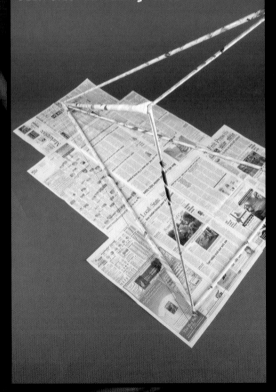

15. Cut a smaller triangle out of a single sheet of newspaper and tape it at the top of the remaining side of the pyramid to allow an opening.

AXIOM ALTERNATIVE

Compare your pyramid's strength to other newspaper shapes. Try building a cube-shaped structure with the same size base as your pyramid. Which structure is stronger?

LOCK AND DAM

Dams on rivers can harness energy to create electricity. They also control water levels to help boats travel safely. But the water levels on opposite sides of a dam often differ by many metres. How do boats safely move from one water level to the other? The answer is a **lock** system. Float your own miniature boat through a lock and dam system to see how it works.

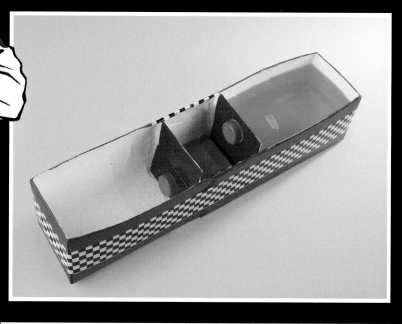

YOU'LL NEED

2 clean 1.75-litre juice cartons with screw cap lids

strong scissors

ruler

packing tape

foam earplug

PLAN OF ACTION

1. Carefully cut off the glued seam on the top of one of the cartons.

2. Open the carton top. Lay it on its side with the spout facing upwards. Carefully cut away the top panel with the spout attached.

3. Repeat steps 1 and 2 with the other carton.

4. Lay one carton inside the other with their bottoms opposite each other to form a larger rectangular box. Overlap the cartons by about 5 cm.

5. Tape the cartons together with strips of packing tape. Tape along the inside overlap and the outside overlap to make the box watertight.

6. Lay one of the pieces of cut away cardboard (with the spout attached) flat. Measure and mark a line parallel to, and 18 cm from, the end nearest the spout. Cut along this line.

lock area of water with gates at both ends; locks help boats move from one water level to another

continued

7. Measure and mark another line parallel to, and 10 cm from, the end nearest the spout. Bend the spout forwards at this line, creasing it at a 90-degree angle.

8. Stand this piece of cardboard inside the box. Place it 19 cm from one end of the box. The spout should face away from the 19-cm section that you just created. Tape the cardboard in place along all sides to make it watertight.

9. Lay the other piece of cardboard (with the spout) flat. Measure and mark a line parallel to, and 10 cm from, the end nearest the spout. Cut along this line.

10. Place this cardboard piece upright inside the box 8 cm from the previous piece. The spout should be near the bottom of the box. It should also face in the same direction as the other spout. Tape this cardboard piece in place along all sides.

11. Cut the foam earplug in half lengthways to make a small boat.

12. With the lids on each of the spouts, place the earplug in the first compartment that you constructed. Fill this compartment to the top with water. Unscrew the lid to this compartment. Notice how the water level becomes equal in the first two compartments. Gently push the boat through the spout into the second compartment.

13. Unscrew the lower lid. Allow the water level to equalize with the lower pool so that the boat can move to the third compartment.

14. To send the boat back upstream, move the boat back to the middle compartment and close the lower lid. Add more water to the first compartment to move the boat back to the higher water level.

15. Adjust the water levels and repeat.

⚡ AXIOM ALTERNATIVE

A river has continuously flowing water that refills each pool as each gate opens. Attach a hose and drain to the system to provide a continuous stream of water to better represent an actual river system.

Glossary

abutment part of a structure that directly receives thrust or pressure

flange lip or edge that sticks out from something

flood plain area of low land near a stream or river that becomes flooded during periods of heavy rain

lock area of water with gates at both ends; locks help boats move from one water level to another

parallel side by side at an equal distance between all points

perpendicular describes two lines that intersect at a 90-degree angle; two lines that form the letter T are perpendicular to each other

septic system drainage system with a tank used to treat waste water

trapezium shape with four sides, only two of which are parallel

trough long, narrow channel

truncate shorten by cutting off the top of an object

Read More

Buildings and Structures (Sci-Hi: Science and Technology),
Andrew Solway (Raintree, 2012)

Buildings (Design and Engineering), Alex Woolf
(Raintree, 2014)

Pyramid (DK Eyewitness), James Putnam
(Dorling Kindersley, 2011)

The World's Most Amazing Bridges (Landmark Top Tens),
Michael Hurley (Raintree, 2012)

Websites

www.bbc.co.uk/education/topics/zvc76sq
Find out more about some real-life engineering projects,
including how engineers solved the "Millenium Bridge
wobble"!

**www.tomorrowsengineers.org.uk/Careers_resources/
Engineering_activities**
Try out these engineering projects from Cargo Drop to Heat
Exchange, to see how science and engineering is applied in
the real world.

Index